Walking with Jerry:

Our family's journey
with our Dad who had
Alzheimer's Disease

By: Helene Harris

Introduction

I am writing this book not only as a tribute to my Dad, Jerry, but to all people who are diagnosed with Alzheimer's disease, as well as their caregivers and family. Watching my father succumb to the cruelties of this condition was not only stressful, but heart-wrenching. This is the story of my wonderful father, Jerry.

Chapter I

Jerry's Early Years

My father, Jerry, was born in Chicago in 1926. Since I believe that a person's childhood has an impact on their lives, it is important that I share his childhood. My father always said he had a tough childhood. He grew up during the Depression. Although my grandfather did have a job, money was still tight. My father said that my grandparents shared their food with others in the apartment complex where they lived. My grandfather worked for the Brach's Candy Company and my father can remember him coming home from work with a little bit of candy that he would give to the neighborhood kids. What was the hardest part of my father's childhood is that his sister, my aunt, had a mental illness. Back in the 30's and 40's mental illness had a negative stigma on the person and family. My grandparents had a hard time not only emotionally, but physically managing a child who at times was violent. As a young child, I knew my aunt had issues, but never understood exactly the problem. My parents shielded my brother and I from any knowledge of my aunt's condition. My Dad always said, "she is not well." Now, as an RN, I know that my aunt most likely had a diagnosis of bi-polar disorder. Even though my aunt never had a formal diagnosis, her symptoms were congruent with typical symptoms of a person with bi-polar disease. Back then, there were not any medications to treat a person diagnosed with bi-polar illness. The mode of treatment back then was "shock treatments". Shock treatments then was crude and non-therapeutic. In some cases, it made the person's symptoms worse. My aunt was given these "shock treatments". They were not beneficial to her. According to my dad, they made her, "more difficult". Dad always said that my grandparents struggled with her. My grandfather would come home from work, eat his supper and escaped by going to pool halls. This situation evidently had a strain on my grandparent's marriage. Dad never really talked much about his childhood, except to say." it was hard." Even with all this happening at home, my father loved school and was popular. Even as a young person, he loved being around people and was extremely social. In high school he played softball on a league. He would tell stories about coming home from school, eating a snack, and then going out to play softball until dark. He also remembered taking his mother to the store pulling his red wagon behind him. He loved his parents and other family members and never caused any serious problems. He essentially was a good kid. My father had three passions: 1) dancing, 2) singing &3) eating. I will discuss the food aspect later in this book. He loved to dance. He always reminisced about going to the Aragon Ballroom (a dance hall where big bands also played) on Saturday nights. My Dad was actually a very good dancer. Jerry completed his childhood happily with fond memories of his grammar school, Goudy School and his beloved high school, Senn High School. To his dying day he praised both of his schools. In 1944 my Dad graduated from his adored Senn High School.

Chapter 2

The Navy Years

My grandfather, my father's father, served his country in the Army in World War (I). He was in the trenches in France. He was exposed to mustard gas throughout his time in the War. When my dad graduated from high school, we were in the throes of World War (II). My grandfather, because of his experiences in the Army, encouraged my dad to join the Navy. My father did just that and in 1944, right after he graduated, he joined the U.S. Navy. In fact, he told a story about how the Navy wanted him to join before he graduated high school. My Dad and grandfather went to the recruiter who agreed to allow my dad to finish school. The day after he graduated, dad was sworn in. He went to basic training at Great Lakes near Chicago. After that he was assigned to an LST-900 ship in the Pacific. LST stands for Landing Ship Tank. It carried cargo and equipment to be unloaded in areas where there were not any docks. My Dad loved his military time.

I can remember about him telling us how "great the food was". I discussed earlier that my dad loved food. I think in some ways, he lived to eat!!!

Anyway, he relished in his time in the Navy. I recall him telling a story. He was in Guinea. His ship was docked not too far from shore. He saw some huts near the beach. He was only 18 at this time, so his young curiosity prompted him to go into one of the huts. Hanging on a string were several shrunken heads. Dad started to take one to bring back to Chicago. As he turned around, he saw a Native Guinean with a machete in his hand. Dad ducked him, ran out of the hut, into the Pacific and back to his ship, He said he did not leave his ship until it docked in Australia!!!

Dad also talked about the time he was "swabbing the deck." He heard planes overhead. The actually were Japanese Kamikaze pilots. He said the plane flew lover over his LST. Everyone on deck just froze, including Dad. Then the plane headed away from the LST. It went in a different direction. A few minutes later, Dad said he saw a "ball of fire" in the distance. The Kamikaze plane flew into another naval ship. Dad said this was really a defining moment in his young life. Dad left the Navy in late 1946. Up until his dying day, he was proud he served his country. When we would be walking around Chicago and dad would see a sailor, he would always state, "I could kick myself for not making a career of the Navy" His commander encouraged him to stay in, but at that time, Dad wanted out. I sometimes wish he had made a career of the Navy. It would have eased his financial issues later in his life. But my Dad had this one mantra: "Never look back. Look forward and learn from your past. Don't dwell, move on." Those words still remain with me to this day.

Chapter 3

Happy and Sad Times

After my dad completed his service, he sold jewelry. In 1949 he married my wonderful mother, Eleanor. My brother was born in 1956 and I in 1952. They had a very happy marriage. Money was tight, but we never knew it. My parents bought a townhouse in Skokie and lived there happily. My parents were very social and had a core group of friends they socialized with. They went dancing and to shows most Saturdays. My parents belonged to a charity organization called the Jenny Singer League for Children. It benefitted sick kids at Michael Reese Hospital. Every year at the end of May or early June my parents and all the other members of Jenny Singer would put on a benefit to raise money. This was a huge production that was held at Nippersink Manor in Wisconsin. This was huge production with costumes, dancing and singing. My parents sang and danced. They always raised quite a bit of money for the hospital. My dad always looked forward to performing. They continued performing in this event until my mother was diagnosed with metastatic breast cancer in 1978.I did not know anything about her diagnosis. I was on active duty stationed in Hawaii. It wasn't until I went on leave that she told me. Unfortunately, her cancer spread to her colon and eventually her liver. My dad had a hard time watching his once vibrant wife go downhill so fast. My mother could no longer live in our townhome, so she moved in with her mother in an apartment. Dad went to see her every day, but he just couldn't handle it. She passed in 1983. Dad was sad, but in some ways, relieved. My husband and I were on active duty. My brother was in graduate school. Neither of us could or wanted to return to Chicago. We both were worried about dad, but had no choice but to leave him in his beloved townhouse. After burying my mom, Dad told my brother and I, "we will continue as a family." I love you guys." Dad always, always, always had a positive attitude. He also instilled that in us. "Think positive", he always said.

I know that many people will say this, but we truly did have the best Dad. Dad was even-tempered, kind, and rationale. He instilled a good value system in my brother and I. When the rare times occurred that my brother and I deserved a spanking, Dad would take off his belt and say, "one, one and a half, two, two and a half, two and three quarters, three." He hated swatting us. His swats never hurt, but my brother and I were embarrassed and disliked disappointing our parents. Dad was just an all-around good guy who loved the Lord and cared about others. He put God and his family first. He worked like a dog to support us. His income was solely dependent on commissions. I believe Mom went to work because Dad's income alone was unable to support the four of us. Dad drove six days a week from our suburb, Skokie, which is on the north side of the city all the way down to the south and west side of Chicago in all types of weather. His work ethic was unsurpassed.

Chapter 4

Jerry, the Widower

After mom's passing, my Dad's friends rallied around him. He met a woman friend that he was with for almost 20 years, but did not want to remarry. He continued to live in his townhouse. Unfortunately, dad was not handy and the townhouse fell into disrepair. Neither my brother nor I knew that he was in severe financial straits. He never would tell us. When we went to Chicago to see him, we were dismayed at the state of the home. My husband Bill, became my dad's "handyman", but again we were both on active duty. Bill would come up once a year to make repairs. Everyone else in the area we lived maintained their townhouse—not my Dad. He was always proud that , " I am an original owner, I've never had to replace anything, my house is in good shape" No, it was not.

Dad worked until he was 75 years old as a salesman. My brother and I went to visit him often. By the late 1990's both my brother and

I lived in Texas. Dad came down often. I took him often to San Antonio. He loved it there. We would go on the Riverwalk. He loved the music. He also saw a lot of my brother in Houston. My brother, sister-in-law, my husband and I would check on Dad. We made sure he was safe in his townhouse and safe driving. At that point, Dad only lived on social security. He never invested any of his money. When my mom passed, my brother and I gave him the money she left us. Had we known he was not going to invest it, we would not have given it to him, but would have invested it for him.

Back in Skokie, socially he was thriving. He would golf, meet friends for dinner, met another group of veterans at McDonald's every morning. He took out his lady friend every Saturday night and met a friend for dinner every Tuesday. We were thrilled.

Chapter 5

The beginning of Alzheimer's

This section is difficult for me to write. My father's Alzheimer's-related symptoms were atypical, vague and insidious. I believe the first time I noticed anything was way back in the early 90's. Dad would have been in his 70's. He was still driving and mostly seemed coherent. I went on my bi-annual visit to Chicago to check on him. The first inkling something was amiss was with his driving. We went to his car to go eat and I noticed that his passenger side mirror was missing. I asked him what happened. He casually stated, "Someone must have stolen it." That seemed odd, but I dismissed it. Then we went out to eat. After eating, dad backed out and hit the bumper of another car. He proceeded to drive away. This was not my dad. Dad was an honest man, full of integrity and God-loving. If I had done this and attempted to drive off, my Dad would have told me to stop and find the owner of the car. I told dad, "stop

Dad, we need to see if there is any damage". He said,"nah, it is just the bumper." I made him stop. I got out of the car and carefully examined the other car. Luckily, Dad just tapped the bumper, there was not any damage. However, I couldn't help but wonder if he had been hitting other cars when he was driving. I immediately called my brother. He made arrangements to come to Chicago in a month to check on dad. I had to get back to Texas. I called Dad every night. He seemed fine. He was taking his lady friend out on Saturday nights, so I thought, "ok, maybe everything is fine." I did not want to admit that my wonderful father was having issues. In March of 1999, I went to Chicago. I would not let him drive to O'Hare to pick me up, so I took a taxi home. I walked in and found dad crawling on his hands and knees. I asked him what he was doing. He started laughing and said he was looking for something. At this time Dad stopped locking his doors. Both his front door and back door were unlocked all the time. My brother and I questioned him. He said his area was safe. We moved to that area in 1958. We were close to all the families in the first three rows of townhouses. Back then everyone walked into everyone else's home. This was forty years later. Many of the original owners moved. People were living there now that dad didn't know. We became concerned. We tried and tried to get him to lock the doors, but to no avail. This was Dad's actions for about six years. There were changes that were so small that I worried, but was complacent.

Several other behaviors surfaced. One was that instead of sleeping in his bedroom, he started living in his basement. He slept down there on an old futon. He never changed the sheets. The futon smelled bad. He never washed his sheets or blanket. He even ate on his futon. He would not leave his basement except to go out. Another serious change was his clothes. He started wearing dirty clothes. My Dad was always fastidiously clean. He would never have gone out in filthy clothes. His lady friend began complaining to me. Now it occurred to us that there may be a problem. Besides his personal changes, his house was unkempt. He had not made any updates on any aspect of his house. Before my mother became ill, she had plans for a new heating/air conditioning unit. Up until then, we had two window air conditioners. When she passed, Dad did nothing. The house needed an HVAC unit, new windows, new plumbing, new appliances (although dad never cooked, he always ate out). I guess at this point my brother and I were in denial. Another out-of-the ordinary sign was Dad's eating habits. He always was a careful eater. In other words, he took small bites, would not talk while eating and wiped his mouth after eating or dribbling food. It was at this time, we noticed his eating habits had changed. He would begin to dribble food, not only on his mouth, but his hands and elbows. It was like he hadn't eaten in weeks. It was becoming unpleasant to eat with him. Again—in denial.

Probably the worst early sign of mental deterioration occurred at the cemetery where my mom and Dad's parents are buried. My grandfather (Dad's father) was a WWI vet. Dad always tried to go to the cemetery several times a year to place a flag on his father's grave. My brother and I were visiting Dad and we all went to the cemetery. Dad realized that he did not have a flag to place on his father's grave. My brother and I assured him that we would buy one and return to the cemetery during the week so that a flag would be placed on my grandfather's grave. My brother and I were walking around. All of a sudden we see that Dad had a flag in his hand. There was absolutely not a flag in Dad's car. I looked at my brother. We knew

Dad had taken a flag. The only thing I hoped is that Dad maybe found the flag in the road. But, unfortunately, I think Dad took it off of someone else's grave. We questioned Dad as to where he acquired the flag. He said "it was in my car." My brother and I did not know whose grave had the flag. So, there goes my Dad, placing the flag on his father's grave. Dad was very honest and full of integrity—again, not my Dad. My brother and I were nonplussed. We hoped this was a fluke. Both of us had to return to Texas, our lives were there. We left Dad and hoped for the best.

Chapter 6

Getting Worse

One night in early 2004 I received a phone call from his cousin. She told me that Dad's driving is awful and she was not going to ride with him anymore. He had driven her and some of her friends to a wedding. She told me she and her friends were scared to death. His lady friend told me the same thing. My brother and I were at our wits end. Dad had been driving all his life as a salesman. Driving was his life. How do we take away his keys? We pushed this under the rug. My feeling was, "well he is happy." I was however, so worried he would hurt himself or even worse someone else. Well, God was watching out for him. My brother and I came to see him March 2007. He seemed fine. His driving was ok. He told us that he was only driving in his area, never in the city. That made us feel better. We spent the whole week with him. We were going out with his lady friend that Saturday evening. Both my brother and I were leaving the next day to get back to

Texas. Around 1 pm dad went down to the basement to take a nap. Around 3 pm he came upstairs. He was speaking incoherently and put 5 cups of water into his microwave in order to make coffee. I am an RN and my brother is a toxicologist. We knew we had to get him to the emergency room. He was having a stroke and we should have called an ambulance, but instead took him in the car. During the short ride, Dad became belligerent, He was talking speaking unintelligently. As soon as we arrived in the ER, Dad became limp. He was dead weight. Someone came with a stretcher. As soon as ad was placed in room he had a seizure. He was sent for a CT scan. The CT scan did not show any abnormalities. Dad was admitted. My brother and I called our respective bosses to let them know what transpired. Both our bosses were very supportive. The next day, dad was back to being himself. He was alert, oriented and wanted to go home. We begged the doctor to keep in the hospital. The physician agreed. Dad was discharged three days later. He was placed on anti-seizure medication. My brother and I had to return to Texas. We both had jobs and at this point I was in the Army reserves. A home health nurse was assigned to dad. Thankfully, Dad's Medicare covered this. Remember, Dad lived on his social security only. My brother and I insisted that before we left for Texas that Dad use an Alert system. We called the company, explained our situation. The system arrived the next day. We set everything up for Dad. We told him to wear the pendant or have it with him at all times. He agreed. I came back to visit around three months later. He refused to wear the pendant at all. In fact, he couldn't even find it. During this time, he was told not to drive, but I believe he did drive. Neither my brother nor I had the heart to take his car keys. By this time, he was doing so well that his home health was cancelled. Things actually remained status quo. Dad was still socially active. He ate out every day for his dinner. Again, my brother and I did not realize the financial strait he was in. We would soon find out.

Chapter 7

Coming to Texas

In January of 2005, Dad's life took a turn. He had another seizure. Thankfully, he was with friends. He was taken to the ER. My brother and I flew to Chicago. Dad, again, recovered. My brother and I went to speak to his personal physician regarding Dad's driving status. The problem was that if Dad could no longer drive, essentially his life was on hold. He could not socialize, pick up his lady friend or even shop. My brother and I were lost. His doctor said Dad could no longer drive. Driving was Dad's lifeline. We knew for his safety and the safety of others that Dad should not be driving. We also recognized that we had to take his car keys back to Texas. We had the hardest time telling Dad, so we waited until the day we left. The morning that we left we told Dad that we were taking his keys. He was furious! We explained to him that his doctor said he could no longer drive, but we added, "for a while". He then informed us that he had another key hidden and would have a duplicate made. This was not the normal behavior of Dad. He was a very understanding, rationale man. The cab arrived to take us to the airport. We found and took with us the other key. We were both crying as we left Dad. That evening I called Dad. He spoke, but was mad. We did arrange with one of Dad's neighbors to take him shopping. Some of Dad's friends came to pick him up as did one of cousins. This cousin lived in the city and it took him over an hour to reach Skokie. He did see Dad monthly.

A few weeks later Dad called me. His lady friend ended their relationship. Just about this time, a senior apartment complex opened in Temple, TX, where I lived. I went to see it. It would be perfect for Dad. The only issue was that this complex was filling up fast. I called my brother. He told me to put down a deposit. It was time Dad was here with his kids. I called Dad's cousins in Chicago, who both felt he needed to be with us. My brother and I both called Dad and told him about this apartment. We told him we wanted him here with us. I really built up this apartment. It was for seniors, it was subsidized by the State of Texas, so that his rent would be reasonable. It had a dining area, as well as activities. Dad actually was happy to leave Skokie. Both his cousins helped persuade him and in March of 2008. My brother flew to Chicago to bring Dad to Texas.. I need to add here that Dad relinquished his driver's license and gave me the title to his car. He said, since he is a new place, he does not want to drive anymore. Thankfully, he stopped driving in a manner of dignity. It was when I saw Dad every dad every day that the Alzheimer's began manifesting itself.

When my sister-in-law cleaned out Dad's house in Skokie, she found his house to be in gross disrepair (far worse than my brother or I knew) and that he was deeply in debt. He had maxed out five credit cards. Dad did not tell us any of this. I think his financial situation also was a catalyst for his move to Texas.

Chapter 8

Life after Skokie

Ever since my mom passed, Dad had one lady friend. He remained with her until the relationship ended. When we brought Dad to Texas, we moved him into a very nice senior complex apartment. He had a small kitchenette, a large bedroom, walk-in closet, large living room and a large bathroom. It was a nice place. Lucky for Dad, it was a low-income place, partially subsidized by the State of Texas. Anyone who made more than a certain amount annually could not reside there. Perfect for Dad who only had his social security. This complex was wonderful. There was a workout room, coffee bar and lots of activities. Dad was very active. He worked out daily and went to all the dances and other events that performed there. He loved it!

There were numerous other widowers, as well as many widows and divorcees his age that resided there. Dad began immediately to seek out women. This was not my Dad. He was a man that was full of integrity. This was not him, but again we didn't think anything of it. But, I had heard it again when I went to visit him. There was one particular woman, we will call her Jean, whom he was attracted to. Jean was a classy lady. She dressed well and was a quiet lady. She also had a male companion who lived at the complex. This companion also had good etiquette, drove a car and really cared for Jean. Jean's companion was also in the Navy and Dad had many conversations with him regarding their Navy stint. Unfortunately, Dad made an egregious error. He started pursing Jean. Jean told him in no uncertain terms that she would be friends, nothing else. I knew it was time for an intervention because Dad was the "talk of the complex." I told him that she is not the right one for him. I told him to wait, someone will be available for him. At this point there started to be a role reversal. I was the parent, he was becoming the child. Still in denial. About a week later, Dad called me and told me he wanted me to meet someone. He wanted me to take them out. Her same was "Bea". I was actually relieved Dad found someone. "Bea" was much younger than Dad. When I went to the complex to pick them up, "Bea" took me aside.

She said the only reason she was doing this was to talk to me. She absolutely had zero interest in Dad. She wanted to tell him that in front of me. I was not happy at all. We went to the restaurant and she politely told Dad that this was it. She would be his friend, but nothing else. He didn't understand. He kept pursuing her. Eventually she moved out of the complex. As always God is in control. About a month later a woman moved in who was closer to his age, divorced and very, very sweet. Her name was "Gail" . "Gail" and Dad were like two peas in a pod. I need to add here that Dad's eating habits were worsening. He was spilling food all over the place. The food was on his clothes, hands and face. He was also wearing dirty clothes, even though I did his laundry weekly, some-times twice a week. He had certain favorite shirts he wore over and over again. I had a girlfriend who sewed,"Jerry-LST-900 on several shirts, "Jerry-Goudy School-1940" and "Senn High School-1944 for him. He loved these shirts and wore them over and over. He was obsessed over his "Senn High School" shirt, his "Goudy School" shirts. He had to have these shirts. I now was washing his clothes three times a week. I started telling him that his clothes were filthy. He didn't see it or care. Dad had a detached retina in his right eye which left him virtually blind. He had glaucoma in his left eye, so needless to say he had vision problems. The VA wanted to help him to see better by ordering him bifocals, but he refused. The point of all this is that even with the dirty clothes and poor eating habits, Gale remained with him. They would go to all the activities together. He spent every day at her apartment. My brother and I were thrilled. Dad and "Gail" spent almost five happy years together. Gail was wonderful to Dad. Unfortunately, "Gail" was diagnosed with an aggressive form of ovarian cancer and passed away in a matter of a few months. Here is when the Alzheimer's really manifested itself. Right after Gail's passing, Dad was "on the prowl" at the complex for a "lady friend." My understanding from the management was that Dad was really annoying various women. He was being ostracized. No one sat with him at lunch or in the coffee bar area. His eating habits were now bordering on, I hate to use the term, but disgusting. Food was all over the table, floor, his shirts and his face. He did not realize his eating habits were so bad. This action, coupled with the bothering women at the complex was the beginning of the end of Dad living there. He would go into the areas of the complex with dirty clothes. My husband and

I both told him about this. I started washing his clothes every other day so that he could wear his favorite shirts. My girlfriend made something close to ten more shirts for him. At this point Dad was not my Dad.

We started to realize at this time that Dad was stealing. I had brought Dad to my house for the weekend. He always took items like paper towels or other innocuous things and put them in his little suitcase that he brought with him. We had Dad to our house almost every Saturday night. He liked my husband's cooking and loved my yellow lab, Max. One Sunday after bringing Dad back to his apartment, he called saying that his television was not working. My husband and I went over to see what the problem was. As soon as we walked in we noticed several pieces of jewelry that Dad had taken from my house. My husband kept some of his cuff-links and jewelry in the room where Dad slept. When we were married, my Mom gave my husband a man's thick gold bracelet with his name engraved on it. My husband treasured that piece. On the counter was that bracelet, some Army pins and cuff links. We were appalled. I asked Dad about it. He seemed nonchalant and said, "oh, I was going to give them to people here." I said, "Dad, those belong to

Bill. Mom gave him the bracelet." He didn't even apologize. We gathered up the jewelry pieces and took them home. From that time forward, either my husband or I checked his suitcase when he left my house. The stealing continued. I would notice that instead of using tissue paper, Dad would take paper towels from the men's restroom in the lobby of the complex. He would hide the paper towels in his closet. He probably had over one hundred pieces of paper towels that he took from the men's restroom. Dad had plenty of Kleenex and handkerchiefs. He would wipe his nose using the paper towels. Discussing this situation with him proved pointless. The "procuring" of the paper towels continued. It only got worse. Dad liked to drink coffee. We bought him a microwave oven for his kitchen. Before I continue, Dad went through a microwave oven a year. He would not clean it (Dad did have a cleaning lady that came weekly), but he never cleaned after himself. He would heat up his coffee and t.v. dinners in his microwave He kept leaving his microwave on, which burned out the motor. He also would leave half-opened t.v. dinners in his microwave. He did not remember doing this.

Dad had plenty of coffee mugs. In the coffee bar in the complex, there was donated coffee mugs that the residents can use. They were all kept in a cupboard. One day, I just happened to open one of Dad's kitchen cabinets and found about twenty five mugs that did not belong to him. I knew they came from the coffee bar. I asked Dad about that. He said, "I needed them". Dad never, ever would have stolen anything from anyone. I panicked. I packed them all up in my car and on my way to work the next morning (very early), I took them all back where they belonged. I told Dad that if he needs anything asked my brother or me. In addition to stealing, Dad was giving away his clothes, shoes and other items in his apartment. When we questioned him, he would say, "I don't need these things". He was left with a small of amount of clothes and one pair of shoes. We tried to stop this behavior, but being that we all worked, it was difficult to stop this behavior.

Besides all this, Dad again was just not clean. Garbage was picked up every Monday. Dad would continually not put the garbage bag over the garbage can incorrectly, so ultimately, stuff was spilled on the edges of the bag. He would put the bag outside is apartment for pickup, but the spilled liquids and food was staining the area by his door. Thus far, the management was tolerant of Dad. He was very well-liked, however, he was not maintaining his apartment. His lease states that the management has the right to go into his apartment if they feel there is a safety issue. Well, a notice was left on everyone's door that the management was going to check on some plumbing issues. So in they go to Dad's place. His cleaning lady was just there. Unfortunately, his toilet was not flushed, there were spills on his floor and a smudge of feces on his closet door. Inevitably, I received a phone call from the management. "Don't you think your Dad needs a higher level of care?" The manager started telling me that he was wearing filthy clothes and smelled bad. Dad was always immaculately dressed and was very concerned about his appearance. I was in absolute denial. I called my brother. We wanted to do everything we can to keep him there. We did not want to place him in a long-term-care facility. The manager suggested having some home health facility come to assist him. I went to talk to Dad's doctor at the VA and told him what was going on with Dad. He approved the need for a home health agency. The social worker assigned to Dad was on top of the situation. The next week, Dad was approved for partial payment for this. Remember, Dad only lived on social security. The Visiting Angels program started the following week. Dad had an aide come three times a week to help him shower and dress. He still insisted on putting on dirty clothes, so I came by every day after work to pick up his clothes. Things were stable for about two months. Besides his aide and cleaning lady, his apartment looked pretty good. The problem was as soon as they left and Dad spilled something he would not clean it up. This was particularly evident in his refrigerator. He would spill liquids (he never recapped anything after he opened it) all over the fridge and onto the floor. My husband suggested putting thick blue pads on each shelf of his refrigerator to absorb the spills. So that is what I did. All of Dad's shelves were lined with thick blue pads. My husband and I cleaned every day also. When my brother and his wife came to see Dad, they too cleaned. We did the best we could in order for him to remain there. During this time, Dad was forgetting to take his evening medications and was careless with his daytime, meds. He had a seizure in the early 2000s, but recovered fine. He was placed on Dilantin for his seizures. Dad was always meticulous about taking his meds. I started noticing that he was forgetting to take his meds because there would be some on the floor and in his sink. I bought him mediation containers and filled them weekly for him. I bought a blue one for his day meds and pink for night. Since Dad's vision was so bad, I wrote in big black letters, "day" and "night". He was still skipping meds. I called the Visiting Angels to see if Dad's aide could make sure he took all his meds. She could not give them to him, but could watch him take them. I told Dad to wait to take his meds until his aide came. I think he found this as an affront. He continued to take his own meds. It was a balance act in allowing Dad to maintain his independence in spite of his decline. Dad was a tough cookie. He fractured his hip in 2013 and recovered fine, but was placed on a walker. Dad, at first managed the walker fine. We so wanted him to live his life.

Chapter 9

Jerry Worsens

Here's where it goes downhill fast for Dad. My husband and I were out and I received a phone call. Dad had fallen in the coffee bar. The management called 911. My husband and I rushed over there. The EMS people were trying to evaluate him. He refused to allow them to touch him and was focused on eating a chocolate chip cookie. He had chocolate all over his hands, face and elbows. Dad had now been in the complex almost five years. Besides this, Dad had caused some angst in the dining hall, He was upset because he did not get an extra piece of cake. The cook told him that if there were any left overs. She would give it to him. Well, Dad used the "f- you word." Dad never said the "f" word. The "f" word was not allowed in our home   Of course the cook had to report this to the management. The cook called me and told me about this. She felt very bad. She really liked Dad, but his behaviors in the dining room were getting worse. He was spilling food all over the place and always wanted more. Dad had plenty of food in his apartment, plus the fact that we took him out to eat weekly and he came to my house every Saturday. Dad ate well. Anyway, she told me, she had no choice but to report this situation to management. I told her that I understood. I called my brother. We knew his lease would not be renewed. I loved my Dad, but he could not live with us. We worked and unfortunately could not handle him. Dad began to get angry at inconsequential things. Surprisingly, he was not yet evicted. Dad originally had his apartment on the second floor, but due to construction issues in the shower, water was leaking and mold developed. Dad was moved to an apartment on the third floor. Besides all of this, other signs that went unnoticed was that dad would use his socks as a handkerchief, even though he had about twenty handkerchiefs. When I talked to Dad about this he just seemed unfazed and kept using his socks in place of handkerchiefs. Again, we just didn't think anything of this. His teeth—Dad had dentures. He was continually losing them. He could not remember where he put them. One time he called me about his lost dentures. I looked and looked and found them in his bed. Another time they were in his kitchen closet. But, through this,

Dad was still basically Dad, so I brushed this off. In addition, Dad called one day panicking. He could not find his wallet. Again, we looked and looked. My husband happened to spot a bulge in his pants. This was a day when his Visiting Angel aide did not come so Dad dressed himself. Dad put his pants on backwards so that his wallet was inside of his pants. I just laughed this off. At this time, also Dad stopped wearing his underpants. He just refused. His Visiting Angel aide tried, but he became angry with her, so she stopped. We tried, but to no avail. Due to this, he was leaking urine in his pants, He also did not wipe himself well after having a bowel movement. Dad just smelled awful. This again, generated more complaints.

I also remember at this time, Dad became infatuated with musicals from the 1930's He constantly talked about Fred Astaire, Ginger Rogers, Gene Kelly, Donald O'Connor, Jimmy Cagney, Jimmy Stewart, Frank Sinatra, and the list goes on and on. One day when I went to see Dad after work, he was alone in his apartment. The t.v. was off and he was sitting in his chair just singing songs from old movies. He liked to sing, "Singing in the Rain and Give My Regards to Broadway", and especially "Yankee Doodle Dandy". He did not know I was there until I said something. Then he laughed and said, "I could have made it in show business. There is no business like show business." This was a theme that would continue to his dying day.

A widow named "Pearl" moved into the complex. It just so happened that his new apartment was right next to "Pearl's" apartment. Dad befriended "Pearl". Their relationship was fairly one-sided. Now Dad was always a kind, giving person. Not so with "Pearl". He became demanding, He would knock on her door at 4 am and insist she cook him oatmeal. At this point he was not only scaring her, but would lash out at her and others. He was still causing angst in the dining room. So, I received another phone call from the manager. The manager told me that he now will need a full- time person with him when he left his apartment. My brother and I did not know what to do. I was told that Dad had to have a full-time caregiver. This was not "assisted living, it is an apartment." The manager also told me that other residents were complaining about Dad's eating and dressing habits. He also had an odor due to his incontinence. I called the Visiting Angels to remind them to have Dad's aide change his clothes when she came every three days and try again with the underpants. He still refused to wear underpants. She actually tried to hide Dad's clothes until I could pick them up. Meanwhile, "Pearl" came over every day, but confided to my sister-in-law that she was afraid of Dad. He was getting very mad over little things. This was not my Dad. All these more consequential behaviors began occurring in October of 2014.

While my brother and I were trying to figure out what the next step was (I was sure at this point Dad's lease would not be renewed in May), the manager called me one afternoon. Dad had a seizure in the coffee bar and had to be taken to the VA hospital. Dad's seizure was bad. He had seizures in the past. He had one about six months earlier when he was eating out with my brother and sister-in-law. His physician told us that Dad could no longer live independently. Our hearts were broken. Neither my brother nor I could care for Dad. If he fell, we could not lift him. The physician said Dad would have to go to a long-term-care facility. My brother and I both knew that, but were crestfallen.

Chapter 10

The End of Jerry's Independence

December of 2014 was the beginning of the end of Dad's life. I wish, wish, wish, I could have Dad in my home during his last years, but that was not feasible. Dad was becoming increasingly irrational and angry. He had also fallen several times. I loved my Dad to death, but again, his personal hygiene was poor. We were renting a duplex and absolutely could not have feces smeared everywhere. My brother and his wife lived in a one bedroom apartment in Houston. Living with them was not an option for Dad. Fortunately, in Temple is a VA long-term-care facility. It is specifically for veterans and their dependents. I figured that since Dad treasured his time in the military, that interacting with other vets would be ideal for him. I went to visit it and was very impressed. It was clean, the food smelled wonderful, the staff was awesome and there were lots of daily activities. In addition, it was about only five miles from my home. It worked for me. I called my brother. He came up to visit the facility. It was hard for him. No matter how good it looked, it is still a nursing home. Now came the hard part—telling Dad. Dad was still in the VA hospital at this point. My brother and I went into Dad's room and trying to maintain his dignity, we told him that because of his seizures, it would be better for him if he went to another "complex" that was for veterans. We told him about the food, the activities and the other WWII vets. Thankfully he agreed. I think Dad was afraid of falling again. Even though he had the Visiting Angels three days a week and "Pearl" right next door, he was becoming more unstable as far as his mobility was concerned. "Pearl" was not coming over to Dad's as much. She was not well herself and could not handle Dad's mood swings. We did not have to tell him that most likely he was going to be evicted from his apartment. The VA hospital staff was great. By the next day, Dad was in the VA State Home.

Dad had a room in the "C" Hall, which was a hall for residents who were more independent. Dad's bed was right next to the bathroom and he had the window side. It was very nice. I forgot to add that since Dad's fractured hip, he began using a walker. He very much relied on his walker. When Dad first received his walker, he used it well. He kept the walker close to his body and did not have any problems. As time went on, he began pushing the walker farther from the center of his body, which meant he was straining his back. The wonderful staff at the VA State Home noticed this and sent Dad to physical therapy (PT) every day. They wanted him to be as independent as possible. Dad seemed to adjust well to the VA State Home in terms of eating and attending the activities, but socially he would not associate with anyone. There were so many men his age that wanted to befriend him, but Dad became "snooty". I really thought that because Dad was a people-person that he would interact with men his age, but he stayed by himself. When playing Bingo, Dad would sit alone, even when asked by others to sit with them. Dad had a wonderful roommate who tried to talk to Dad, but Dad was not interested. His roommate told me that Dad would walk away when the roommate tried talking to him. I think Dad turned many people away. He was telling staff and his roommate that he was a Broadway star. Some people believed him, some questioned him, but he told his roommate he was a Broadway star plus the men he sat with. I believe people were unimpressed.

We tried to give Dad all the comforts of home. We bought him a television, telephone and a small refrigerator. Dad was on a Pepsi binge. He would drink at least 3-4 small bottles of Pepsi a day. Well I take that back—he would take sips out of 3-4 small Pepsis a day. We stocked his refrigerator with plenty of Pepsi. Every weekend, I would stock him up. Unfortunately, he kept spilling the drink in his refrigerator and on the floor. This was an ongoing battle with Dad about making sure he puts the lids back on. I felt bad for the housekeepers. They were constantly in Dad's room cleaning the floors and his refrigerator. Dad's roommate had very poor vision and the last thing we wanted was for him to fall while going to the bathroom. Again, I would put towels on the inside of the fridge in an attempt to sop up the liquid. This was another ongoing issue. I came over every day after work to clean the fridge.

I need to add that every Saturday I came to take Dad to my house. He loved watching old movies. He liked the way my husband made bacon and eggs, so that was his Saturday ritual along with a chocolate milk shake. The routine was the same every Saturday. He liked to watch the same films over and over again. This was his enjoyment, so it became my enjoyment. My brother and his wife came from Houston to see Dad monthly. They would take him out to eat, but once he was wheelchair bound, that became difficult, so they always brought him food. Dad was very much loved by his kids.

After about six months, Dad was becoming less and less my Dad. I absolutely do not attribute this to the VA State Home, but to Dad's exacerbation of Alzheimer's. Dad was assigned a table in the dining hall with three other veterans, two of whom were also WWII vets. Dad always came to the dining room about one hour before meals were served. He would go in his wheelchair over to the coffee area and bring himself two cups of coffee, which he never drank. He would sit there alone. He ate at this table for about three months. Then the complaints began. Dad's eating habits were alienating him. No one at the table wanted him sitting there anymore, so he was moved to another table. That lasted less than one month—again complaints about his eating habits. Always trying to maintain his dignity and leave him in the dining hall, the staff placed him at a table with veterans who had some dementia and who required close watching. Dad ate at that table until he was moved to the locked unit. No one at that table cared about Dad's eating habits.

During this time, Dad refused to continue with physical therapy. He said he "graduated". This was not the case. The PT staff ordered him a new walker thinking that maybe he would walk better. He was very unstable on his walker because he held so far ahead of his center of mass. Unfortunately for Dad, he fell two times in one week due to misuse of the walker. The nurses were concerned and placed Dad in a wheelchair for a few days with the understanding that after more PT that he would return to his walker. This never happened. Dad checked himself out of PT and right into the wheelchair. No convincing of us or the staff would change his mind. "I graduated from therapy and I am in a wheelchair, period". That is what he would say. "I am doing my exercises, see, I am wheeling myself down the hall." The staff wanted Dad back in physical therapy not just for mobility but also for cognitive therapy. They had him doing puzzles and other word games to ensure maximum cognitive thinking. However, Dad refused to return to PT and finally he was dropped from the program. This "wheelchair" situation made it difficult to bring Dad to my house. I was able to get Dad from the wheelchair to the car, as well as placing the wheelchair in the trunk by myself. Getting the wheelchair with Dad in it into my house was more difficult. My husband helped me to navigate the wheelchair into our house. It was not easy. Dad would settle into a chair for the first few months, but after that remained in the wheelchair

My Dad who was a salesman interacted with people of different ethnicities every day. He was not a prejudiced person at all. In fact, when my mom passed away one of Dad's customers, who was a Palestinian, invited Dad over to his home for dinner every week. Dad continued this tradition for years and years. The reason I am writing about this is because Dad started belittling some of the African-American aides. He would call them the "N" word and also started using the "f" word. This was so not my Dad. If he had been lucid this never would have occurred. In reality, if he had known what he was saying, he would be mortified. I came to see him and he was calling a very sweet African-American aide a "N". I was sick. I couldn't believe he was saying that. I would have gotten the belt if I came home and said that. The staff told me to go home, "he was not having a good day." Due to his increasing agitation and combativeness, Dad was placed on Ativan (a medicine that calms him down, but also made him drowsy). The staff tried to curtail the Ativan use, but Dad was now receiving it at least twice a day.

Another day I came to see him, I found him in his closet. He was obsessed with his LST-900 and his Senn High School shirts. He was panicked because he could not find them and insisted someone stole them. They were not stolen. The staff had to place his dirty clothes in a separate room. If his dirty clothes were in his laundry basket, he would remove his clean clothes and put on a dirty shirt. I came every other day to pick up his laundry. I tried explaining this to him. He was not comprehending and continued to complain that his clothes were being stolen.

During all this, Dad still came over to my house on Saturdays if the Staff determined he was not agitated. If he was, I would be told to go home and see him another time. When he became agitated (again, so not my Dad), he would be given Ativan, which made him sleep for hours. Both my brother and I had a hard time—this was not kind-hearted, easy-going Jerry.

Even at my house, Dad was not my Dad. One day he was watching a movie. In an instant, he turns his head to the wall and says the names of his schoolmates and some of his childhood haunts in Chicago. The he says "and Jerry was there too." I started to become very concerned. My husband suggested taking him back to the VA State Home. Dad was falling more and more into Alzheimer's. When I told the nurses what had happened, they agreed that bringing him back was the right thing to do. When I went to see Dad on Monday, his Hospice nurse was there. Dad was in the dining room going back for this third cup of coffee (he hadn't even taken a sip from the other two cups on his table). The nurse said, "the man in the wheelchair is your Dad physically, but not mentally." He was right.

Dad's agitation was worsening. My Dad was absolutely the nicest man. I came in and saw him talking with the Hospice nurse. Dad's hospice nurse checked on Dad at least twice a week. I came to see Dad around lunch time and Dad was, I thought, talking to his Hospice nurse. As I came closer Dad said to him, "f-you, leave me alone." The Hospice nurse told me to go home. I felt very bad. This was 100% not my Dad. Growing up I can't even count on one hand the time Dad became mad at my brother or I. The extremely few times that he did were warranted. Again, the "f" word was not in Dad's vocabulary.

In the midst of all this, Dad was having a refrigerator issue. Dad blew out his first refrigerator after only six months of residing at the VA State Home. Dad would not close the door on the fridge, liquid kept spilling on the floor as well as the table on which Dad's refrigerator was placed. Refrigerators can only take so much abuse. After only six months the motor stopped. Due to all the misuse of the refrigerator, plus the safety issues for Dad and his roommate, my brother and I were tempted not to buy Dad another one, but he was insistent that he needed one. Like many families who are forced to make the difficult decision to place a loved one in a long- term care facility, my brother and I felt guilty. We caved and the next day Dad had a new refrigerator. The refrigerators we purchased were small enough to be placed on a side table. Again, the inside of the fridge was lined with towels as well as placing a towel underneath the fridge in an attempt to sop up any spilled liquid. The misuse of the refrigerator continued on for another six months. Not only did Dad have Pepsi and water in there, but he would bring two to three cups of juice from the dining room after each meal. There wasn't any room and again liquid was spilled all over everything. In addition, the soda pop was sticky. Dad's area was always a sticky mess. The poor housekeepers were mopping up his area at least three times a day.

As patient as the staff was towards Dad's refrigerator issue and as accommodating as they can be, the plug was pulled on Dad's refrigerator. I was called in by the head nurse on Dad's hall as well as Dad's hospice nurse. The fridge had to go. It was becoming more and more of a safety issue, plus the stickiness was attracting bugs. I called my brother, he concurred. The staff, though has two large refrigerators behind the nurses' station. They agreed to reserve part of one refrigerator for Dad's soda pop and juices. All Dad had to do was ask and he could have his drinks whenever he wanted. Now came the hard part—telling Dad. When Dad was at lunch the refrigerator was removed and placed in my car. The staff graciously took the responsibility of telling Dad. He was told a little white lie (which really was not too far from the truth). He was told that the refrigerator broke and had to be removed. Of course, I received a phone call from Dad. He was very upset. He wanted his refrigerator back. I explained to him that it was broken and being repaired. I have never lied to my Dad, but he would have not understood the real reason for the removal of his refrigerator. I told Dad, "Dad, you have a refrigerator, it is in the nurses' station. All you have to do is ask for a Pepsi and the nurses will give you one. Dad then called my brother who corroborated this story. This was again was not far from the truth. This second refrigerator was on its last leg. The staff was extremely accommodating. When I would visit Dad, he would have two to three Pepsis and juice cups on his bedside stand. Soon, Dad realized that he still had access to his drinks. I stocked the nurses' station fridge with Pepsis'.

I think out of all the changes in my wonderful Dad, caused by Alzheimer's, the worst was yet to come.

Chapter 11

The beginning of the end for Jerry

During all these changes, I still brought Dad to my house on Saturdays. It was becoming increasingly difficult due to his inconsistent outbursts and the worse—he refused to wear any type of undergarment so he was continually leaking urine and stool. This began about the same time his dementia was also worsening. The staff tried to encourage him to wear Depends, but Dad refused. So, unfortunately, coupled with all the other disturbing habits, he smelled all the time. At times, his stool was so loose that it leaked down his pants and onto his shoes. Dad had been fastidiously clean. This was not him. It was hard to take him to my rental home, as well as it was hard for my brother and his wife to take him to a restaurant. I had to Lysol my car seat, furniture and floor after I took him back to the State Home. I think that this situation contributed to his alienation at the State Home. But, bless the staff, they tried.

We felt terrible for Dad's wonderful room-mate. There was always stool on the com-mode seat. Again, housekeeping practically lived in Dad's room.

Here are one of the three worst changes in Dad. I came to see him one Sunday. He was sitting in his room in his chair. When I came in he said, "I'm getting married next week and need $200.00." I tried to be nonchalant about it. I asked Dad who this woman was. He said, "she is a Mexican woman." I did not know how to answer him, so I said, "let's talk to Fred (my brother). He became livid. "Why do you have to call him?" I'm getting mar-ried and I want $200.00. It's my money and I want it." Before I continue, I need to add that Dad always kept a "stash" of $200.00 in his home for "emergencies". He was in-sistent on keeping money in his room, even though he did not need it. That was an ongo-ing battle. Finally, my brother and I conceded and put a $10.00 bill in one of his drawers. By next week it was gone. We, at that time, convinced Dad if he needed any money, all he had to do was ask. That solved that situation for a while, or so we thought. So, getting back to this "marriage" situation, Dad started yelling at me about his "marriage and money." The staff heard this conversation and called the social worker. Dad told her that, "my daughter doesn't believe me." I am getting married (now he said "next month", earlier it was, "next week"). The social worker did her best to calm him down, but to no avail. Dad was given an Ativan and I went home. During my drive home, Dad called my husband. He told Bill, my husband, that he was mad at me and that I didn't believe him about getting married. He then hung up. Following the social worker's and staff's advice, I stayed away from Dad for two days. In the meantime, I asked the staff if anyone came to see him besides my brother and I. They were adamant. Dad did not have any other visitors. They were aware of Dad's comments and said they would keep an eye out for any other visitors. Of course, no one else visited Dad. After about a week, this situation was history.

However, another one cropped up. Dad was insistent that he wanted a female "companion". He would ask the staff for paper so that he can write "advertisements" for a 65 year-old female companion. First off Dad was 89, secondly, the VA State Home does not have companions. If I wanted to, I could contact the Visiting Angels to send someone to sit with him, but that would have to come out of Dad's low- income status. Dad's social worker was concerned that even if we did contact the Visiting Angels for a "sitter" that Dad would want her there all the time. The staff and social work were also concerned about Dad becoming angry with her when she left. This unfortunately was an ongoing problem until he passed away. Dad insisted that my sister-in-law and I find him someone. He said, "I am counting on you to find me a lady friend with big breasts. She is going to have to move in with me." After talking with the Hospice nurse and social worker, I was instructed to tell Dad, "we are looking for someone for you Dad." That was my standard answer every time Dad brought up the "companion/lady friend" issue. My sister-in-law told him the same thing, "we are looking, Jerry."

While all this was going on, we started to have a "telephone issue". Dad would call me at least five times a day to talk about his "companion" and discuss his friends from the past. He was slipping away every day. He also called my brother very often. About a year after Dad was in the VA State Home, I received a phone call from Dad's hospice nurse. "We have to tell you to remove Mr. Reitman's phone." He called 911 last night and

the EMS team arrived at the State Home."
I came right over. Dad's nurse told me that
around 0200 an ambulance and a police of-
ficer arrived at the State Home. They were
able to trace the 911 call to Dad's room. I
was perplexed. I had no idea that Dad would
even consider calling 911. I was not told what
the 911 complaint was, but only that the EMS
team and the police were upset. I called my
brother. He agreed. While Dad was eating, I
pulled his phone and cancelled his contract.
It broke both our hearts. We told Dad that he
didn't need a phone because I came to see
him every day and Fred came about every
two weeks.

For some reason during all this angst, Dad
was convinced my brother and his wife were
getting divorced. Where this thought process
came from is unknown. But Dad was insistent. No amount of convincing was affecting
this thought. I tried and tried. Dad would
become angry and raise his voice, "they are
getting a divorce, period!", he would say.
Fred and Mildred came to see Dad and told
him that they were happily married. It still
took a few months before Dad dropped this.
In fact, he denied ever saying this.

Also during this time, Dad became very
homesick for Chicago. He kept saying how

much he missed Chicago. This was a repetitive comment. We felt bad. We knew he missed his city, but there wasn't any way he could go back at this time.

For my brother and I, here came the worst. The more Dad was slipping away under the "Alzheimer's spell", the more hypersexual he became. Dad was always a modest, upright man. Sexual conduct is something that was taboo in our house. Now Dad began touching the breasts and the backside of the young aides. Of course, they complained and when it was Dad's turn to shower two aides had to be with him. The Staff knew that this was not Dad. He certainly did not display this behavior until the end. My brother and I were beside ourselves. The Hospice team had to place Dad on estrogen to counter the hypersexuality conduct. The estrogen seemed to work some, but he still displayed that behavior. We were crushed. I was told that this type of behavior was a precursor to Dad having to be moved to the "locked unit" The VA State Home had a unit specifically designed for residents with end-stage dementia as well as those veterans who displayed behaviors that were difficult for the lower-level units to handle.

About a week after Dad's phone situation

and the worsening of his behaviors, Dad's social worker called me at home. Dad had to be moved from his room to the locked unit due to not only his behaviors, but because he was going into other residents' rooms. I asked his social worker if she thought maybe this wandering was due to his getting lost, but we both knew that Dad lived in his room for over a year—he knew his room. The social worker told me they were going to move Dad the next morning and that I should stay away for a few days. I knew this was the beginning of the end for my wonderful Dad. He would no longer be able to wheel himself into the dining hall and get his three cups of coffee. He would no longer attend activities on his own, even though he stopped going, but that was his choice. I called my brother. We were terribly upset, but both of us knew this was an unavoidable choice for the State Home. Now Dad would be with other veterans who had severe dementia.

Chapter 12

Dad goes Home

I complied with the request of Dad's social worker and stayed away for two days, but I did call every night to check on him. The staff was honest, he was not adjusting well. When I went to see him, he was angry. He said, "I am miserable here, I want to go back to room 507. I did not know what to say. It would not have been beneficial to explain why he was moved. He would not understand. The staff was wonderful. The gave Dad all the Pepsis' he wanted. They tried to engage him in activities, but all he did was sit in his room. After about three days in the locked unit, there was a rapid decline in Dad. He began to cough and run a fever. In addition, he was not hungry (my Dad was always hungry). The Hospice nurse called me. Dad's lungs were very congested. Since Dad was on Hospice, it was not recommended that he be treated, just comfort care only be given to him. I called my brother. Due to his poor quality of life, we made the decision for comfort care only for Dad. Let him go to Heaven in peace. Dad was treated with medication to loosen the congestion and ease the cough, but antibiotics were not ordered for my Dad. I went at least three times a day to see him. My brother and his wife were coming weekly from Houston. After two days of lying in bed, I went to see Dad and he was dressed and eating, well attempting to eat. He was spilling food all over the place. We watched as Dad was trying to eat his lunch. As I wrote at the outset, eating good food was one of the things he loved doing the most, and now that was all he had left. My brother watched Dad struggling just to eat some soup from a mug, until it became too uncomfortable to watch. The staff at first was feeding him, but then gave him the mug so he could try to eat himself. Dad promptly dropped the mug which spilled the soup all over his lap. Dad stated how miserable he was and began crying. The only time I saw Dad cry was when his parents and my mother passed on. Food was all Dad had left, and now he didn't even have that. That was all my brother could take. He told Dad (correctly) he needed to leave for home and Dad just waved him away. He left the room rather sure that was the last time he would see his father alive.

My brother and I were besides ourselves. We both could not stay because we were both about to cry. My brother said, "this is no life for Dad". I agreed. Thanks, be to God, Dad did not remain in the locked unit long. After only nine days, Dad lapsed into a coma. He was unresponsive for three days. On June 8, 2016, Dad went home to Heaven. He is now dancing with my mom and his family. He is square dancing with my mother-in-law and doing the Irish Jig with my Irish Mum!! He is singing Dancing in the Rain with Gene Kelly and Give My Regards to Broadway with James Cagney!!! Dad always told me, "I love you Babe". Dad I love you and miss you!!!

Summary

We sent Dad back to his beloved city of Chicago. He is laid to rest next to my mother and only a few feet away from his parents and sister. His best friend is also buried not too far from him. Dad had a wonderful send off. Some Navy staff from Great Lakes came and played Taps for Dad. He would have loved this since he was so proud of his Navy stint. Dad is now at peace.

What I learned from this experience is how Alzheimer's totally robbed my Dad of the person he was. There was a total juxtaposition on who Dad was and who he became. This experience brought our whole family closer together and made me more acutely aware of what other families and people afflicted with Alzheimer's manage daily. This was not easy. That is the reason this story is dedicated to caregivers, family members and people who are plagued with this disease. I now donate faithfully to the Alzheimer's Association. We need to find a cure for this dreadful condition.

There are several "Jerryisms" that I will take with me the rest of my life:

1. God and family are always first

2. Always think positive

3. A car is not a toy—take care of your car

4. Business is business-when you are at work, your work is your priority

5. Health is wealth

6. Getting old is not for sissys'

Pictures of Jerry:

1. Jerry leaning against the car in 1980

2. Jerry with me and my brother in 1992

3. Jerry sitting with me in 2015—in the throes of Alzheimer's

Made in the USA
Coppell, TX
04 November 2022

85719827R00039